My Homework Ate My Dog

Great Cartoons from the Phi Delta Kappan, *1991-1996*

Edited by Carol Bucheri and Sheila Way

Phi Delta Kappa International
Bloomington, Indiana U.S.A.

Cover illustration by Dave Carpenter

Book design by Carol Bucheri with production assistance
from Sheila Way, Victoria Voelker, and Terri Hampton

Published by Phi Delta Kappa International, Inc.
408 North Union Street
P. O. Box 789
Bloomington, Indiana 47402-0789
U.S.A.

Library of Congress Catalog Card Number 96-70231

ISBN 0-87367-803-6

Printed in the United States of America

Foreword

As the jack-of-all-trades on the *Kappan* staff, I find that my office often looks like the aftermath of a collision between a bookmobile and an office supply delivery truck. I haven't yet figured out how to pile things on the ceiling, but given that it's the only uncluttered surface left, I may be forced to invent ceiling "sticky files" within the next year. I mention this because I'm sometimes tempted, by the example of all those children in cartoons who blame their missing homework on their dogs, to bring my Cairn Terrier to my office and turn him loose. And while he is quite famous in my neighborhood for having once eaten an entire bowl of Christmas candy (foil wrappers and all) as well as having gobbled up – with no apparent ill effects – a basket's worth of Easter eggs as they were being hidden, I think that even he would be daunted by the mountains of paper on my desk.

But the one stack of papers I always find time for are new submissions from the *Kappan* cartoonists. From Luci Meighan's pig, captioned "I'm pink, therefore I'm Spam," to the dear late Ford Button's "Mom, I need an eagle feather for my science project tomorrow morning," humor provides the leavening that makes our very serious work palatable. Readers let us know how much they value *Kappan* cartoons – rating them highest on every survey we've conducted. So it is with real pleasure that we offer you this selection of cartoons culled from *Kappans* published during the last five years. Our editorial staff – Pauline Gough, Bruce Smith, and Risë Koben; office and production staff – Terri Hampton, Sheila Way, and Debbie Webb; and design staff – Victoria Voelker and I – all participated in the selection process to bring you these very best of *Kappan* cartoons.

Carol Bucheri
Design/Advertising Director and Circulation/Production Manager
Phi Delta Kappan

My Homework Ate My Dog

"It's for the teacher's pet."

"Of course, he only watches educational television."

"The science fair is today, Dad. I'll need your stomach contents."

"I believe this one will go down in science fair history."

"We had some creative differences."

"*I'm not certain, but I believe one of the children must have planted kudzu in the class terrarium before summer vacation.*"

9/94

"*I draw from my kindergarten experiences.*"

"Are you sure Ms. Crawford didn't mean President *Garfield?"*

"*Maybe I should stay home. That might be acid rain.*"

"I hope we have the spelling test early, while I'm still under the influence of my alphabet cereal."

10/94

"He's already learned his ABC's, and now we're working on his DEFGHIJKLMNOPQRSTUVWXYZ's."

12/92

"*Sorry I'm late, Ms. Frankle, but Mom said I was too aggressive at breakfast this morning, and she made me listen to whale sounds for 30 minutes.*"

6/96

17

"*Are you tapping into my computer again, Mom?*"

The No-Passing Zone

"Well, Brooks, I'm giving you a C. I believe this effort deserves an F for ability to follow instructions but an A for realization of full potential."

"How appropriate — absolute zero."

"Son, I want you to feel as if you could ask me about anything — except how to do synthetic division of polynomials."

"*No wonder the kid's exhausted. He's been playing a duet.*"

"*How come Al Gore can reinvent it, and I can't?*"

"Do you sometimes get the feeling that this classroom was designed for older students?"

"After 10 hours of day care, going home to my parents is always a real culture shock."

"And just when I thought it couldn't get any worse, I find out I'm a history teacher."

"I don't think we should have geography for a while — until they decide how many countries there should be."

11/92

"*James, we've talked about this before; the modeling clay is for everyone to play with.*"

"You realize, Paul, that getting an 'A' for your time machine is contingent upon your fixing it and getting us back to Hope Valley High."

"For further information, dial 1-800/I-DO-MATH."

"Take a couple of books out of my backpack."

And Gladly Teach

"Hello, Principal McPherson? This is your second-grade substitute. The kids have filled me in on the routine."

12/95

"*Good morning, girls and boys. I'm old lady Larson, and I'll be your teacher this term.*"

12/95

"I'm not sure what Mr. Ziegler has got planned for class today, but, quite frankly, I'm worried."

10/91

"*Sorry, Ms. Tuttle. We ran out of paper last night, and I had to write my report on sticky notes.*"

3/96

"I feel fat!"

"Yo, Mrs. Wilson! Remember me, Fred Mooney — the one who looked out the window all the time?"

11/93

"*Sure, history's easy for you. You've* lived *it!*"

"For the last time, this is called 'current events,' not 'Headline News.'"

"City children have trouble with the concept of harvest."

10/93

"*You probably noticed by now that I'm not exactly suffering from an intelligence overload.*"

"I can't do big math problems. My calculator doesn't have any numbers higher than nine."

2/94

"What I did on my summer vacation, by Spike Hallinan . . ."

"*My dog* wouldn't *eat my homework!*"

"Sure, I know what the breakup of the Soviet Union means . . . 15 new countries on the geography test."

5/92

"Dr. Robinson, quick! We've got a finger-paint class out of control!"

"I paint what I see."

"I typed my report, but I had to use a lot of Liquid Paper."

"*I know Michelangelo did nudes and Degas did nudes and Manet did nudes. But, as long as I'm the instructor, Billy MacCauley will* not *do nudes.*"

10/94

"*I wish you hadn't used that coffee mug — I had those colors mixed just right.*"

Class Clowns

"No use debating environmental versus genetic causes. Either way, it's your fault."

12/92

"*Do you mind if I use another 'Sesame Street' analogy?*"

"I don't know how I was supposed to find the English Channel. I didn't even have the remote control."
2/94

"I don't have my homework. My dog deleted it."

"What's the job market like for a Nintendologist?"

"*Of course it's wrong. That's why I go to school.*"

"HA! At our school, we don't have to wear uniforms."

"*He's doing the coloring, and I'm doing the color commentary.*"

"Reading is important, Kevin. You need it to understand computer manuals."

9/91

"Will this be on the test?"

12/92

"I think I'm the teacher's pet, Mom. She keeps telling me I'm in her doghouse."

5/95

"And then she said, 'If you like watercolors so much, you learn to do watercolors!'"

"Now I'm confused."

"*Sorry I don't have all my art supplies, Ms. Carmichael. I dropped my bottle of glue on the way to school.*"

"It's the technical support number . . . kind of a homework hotline for grown-ups."

11/94

"*Great! We're just beginning to learn our multiplication tables, and* she *says we need to start thinking about the SAT.*"

"It's okay, Miss Evans — he's a retriever!"

11/91

"What's the scientific expression for 'yucky'?"

"*I'm looking for a book with photographs of cavemen.*"

3/95

"We have him enrolled in one of those alternative obedience schools."

2/95

School's Out

"If you ask me, there's more violence over television than on it."

"Don't be so negative, Mom. Think of it as desktop publishing."

"*Mom, guess what I did in science class today!*"

"*Because Daddy doesn't* want *to know how to write 23 using base 2.*"

"That's a good question, Todd. I'd say apple. Apple or pumpkin."

"*It's the weekend, Mom. Read me one without a moral.*"

"Gee, Dad, it sure is nice of you and your research staff to help me with my homework."

11/91

"*I like the concept, but I think it needs a bit more thought.*"

11/91

"I have a love of words, too."

"*I'm not going to school today. I think I caught a cold from an open window on my computer.*"

4/94

"Hello, Grandma? Wanna come to the Thanksgiving play? I have a real meaty part."

11/92

"*It appears to be an account from the pharaoh's young son, titled 'How I Spent My Summer Vacation.'*"

12/94

"The only country I could identify was Italy."

"The first two weeks are always the hardest — 'Sesame Street' withdrawal."

"I'm playing Santa in the Christmas play. I need a pillow and eight tiny reindeer by Friday."

11/94

"It's for you."

THE
CHILDREN'S
CENTER

"If you must read over my shoulder, Kruptner, kindly refrain from sounding out your letters."

11/92

"See — that's *how he's able to write all those plays."*

"*The human brain starts working the moment you're born, and it doesn't stop 'til you get to long division.*"

12/91

"Their book was on 'Reading Rainbow.'"

Grading on the Curve

Coach Riley was an innovator in the field of basketball recruitment.

11/92

"Boy! If we learn from our mistakes, today should have made me pretty smart."

"You'll never get away with it. She's bound to know it was you, Pablo!"

"This is the week Mr. Conklin teaches aerodynamics."

"*I have a feeling that this is going to be predictable.*"

"Richard, let's have a talk about margins and report lengths."

"*You're getting warmer.*"

"The board has suggested we get back to the Dewey decimal system, Mr. Crocker!"

"*You're still diving too flat, Byron!*"

"Hi, I'm Grant. The government sent me."

"*I'm revising one of the classics to make it more appealing to today's yuppie mentality. I'm calling it* Tom Lawyer *and* Huckleberry Thin.*"

"Well, of course I'm childish and immature — I'm 8."

"I couldn't remember the capital of South Korea to save my soul."

2/93

"They had a substitute. A good time was had by all."

The Cartoonists

George Abbott

A retired postal worker, George Abbott has been cartooning for several years. His wife Marianne helps prepare cartoons for mailing and offers advice and encouragement. Abbott's first big sale was to the *National Enquirer*; since then, his cartoons have appeared in most major magazines and in many trade journals, as well as in several collections. "I do a few, I sell a few," he says. Since retirement he divides his time between cartooning and model railroading.

Charles Almon

Charles Almon received an M.F.A. from Pratt Institute, majoring in painting, after some years as a corporate art director (abstract expressionism had peaked). He is now a full-time cartoonist. The reclusive Brooklyn artist could provide only this 1949 snapshot, taken with his gun-toting brother, Sam, now an attorney. "I look pretty much the same, except I'm taller, bearded, and have a tad more calf-muscle," states Almon.

Donna Barstow

A self-proclaimed TV addict, Los Angeles-based cartoonist Donna Barstow worked at TV and movie studios for several years before turning to cartooning. Her work has been published in a broad range of newspapers, consumer magazines, and business publications in more than 60 major markets. Titles include the *Wall Street Journal*, *National Review*, *Emmy*, *Columbus Dispatch*, *Cosmopolitan*, the *Saturday Evening Post*, *Reader's Digest*, and *Family Circle*.

Ford Button

Jazz guitarist, history buff, and cartoonist for over 30 years, Ford Button, who died this year, was one of the nicest people we've had the pleasure of working with here at the *Kappan*. We'd like to offer a special thank-you to Ford's wife Joyce and daughter Connie for their help in locating cartoons for inclusion in this book. Ford Button's cartoons have appeared in *Good Housekeeping*, the *National Enquirer*, *Better Homes and Gardens*, *Family Circle*, and in many trade, technical, and fraternal magazines.

Photo by Rachel Cotham

Frank Cotham

Cartoonist Frank Cotham has had cartoons published by a number of magazines, including the *New Yorker*, the *Wall Street Journal*, *Barron's*, and the *Saturday Evening Post*. He held a number of jobs before becoming a cartoonist, but he considers cartooning "the most satisfying by far."

Benita Epstein

Benita Epstein's cartoons have appeared in over a hundred books, greeting cards, and magazines — including *Writer's Digest*, *Artist's Magazine*, *American Scientist*, and *Natural History*. She became a full-time cartoonist in 1992 after 20 years spent in conducting scientific research at three universities. She holds a master's degree in entomology and has been co-author of a dozen scientific papers.

Martha Campbell

With a B.F.A. from Washington University, St. Louis, Martha Campbell is a former writer/designer for Hallmark Cards. A freelance cartoonist since 1973, she started when her daughter was 3, she was expecting her second child (a son), and her studio was a closet just wide enough for a drawing board. Now her children are college graduates, and her studio is a full-sized room with a copier, a computer, four file cabinets, and a dog. She lives in Harrison, Arkansas, with the same husband she started out with — and, of course, neither of them has changed at all.

Dave Carpenter

Dave Carpenter started cartooning professionally in 1976, becoming a full-time cartoonist in 1981. He spends two hours a week teaching art at one of the local junior high schools in his area, and he says that with each session "my admiration increases for those in the teaching profession — I salute you!" His cartoons have appeared in the *Wall Street Journal*, *Forbes*, the *Saturday Evening Post*, *Better Homes and Gardens*, *Good Housekeeping*, and a number of other publications.

James Estes

A full-time cartoonist for more than 26 years, Estes numbers among his clients *Good Housekeeping*, the *Wall Street Journal*, *Reader's Digest*, and *Highlights for Children*. He and his wife Martha, who've been married for 32 years, obviously stressed the importance of education to their children — son Robert is a West Point graduate, daughter Kelley has a master's degree in special education, and daughter Paige will complete her education degree in 1997.

Stan Fine

Stan Fine's cartoons have spanned five decades and are still being published in all the major magazines in the U.S. and abroad. He studied at the Philadelphia Museum College of Art and the Hussian Art School before going out to look at the world through cracked rose-colored glasses — and found that he was getting paid for it. Stan is a transplanted Philadelphian now living in Florida with his lovely wife.

Randy Glasbergen

More than 20,000 of Randy Glasbergen's cartoons have been published by *America Online*, *The Funny Times*, *Glamour*, the *Wall Street Journal*, and many others. His comic panel, "The Better Half," is syndicated worldwide by King Features Syndicate. Randy is also the author of several books, including *Technology Bytes!*, *Are We Dysfunctional Yet?*, *Attack of the Zit Monster and Other Teenage Terrors*, *How to Be a Successful Cartoonist*, and *Getting Started Drawing and Selling Cartoons*. He also creates "Today's Cartoon by Randy Glasbergen," which appears exclusively on the World Wide Web. Randy lives in New York State with his family, a bloated poodle, and several deeply troubled cats.

Sidney Harris

As one of the few remaining people trying to communicate without any electronic assistance, Sidney Harris has been stocking up on paper and ink as art supply stores in the New York area drop like flies. The print editions of his two most recent cartoon collections, *There Goes the Neighborhood* (cartoons on the environment) and *Einstein Atomized* (science), are in the stores, but he hopes to get them into cyberspace before the millennium.

Henry R. Martin

Henry R. Martin's cartoons have appeared in many national magazines and newspapers, including *ABA Press*, *American Scientist*, the *Chicago Tribune*, the *New Yorker*, *Saturday Review*, and the *Wall Street Journal*. He has also published a number of cartoon collections. He is currently basking in the pleasures of retirement.

Scott Arthur Masear

Having worked many jobs before finding his calling as a freelance cartoonist, Scott Arthur Masear continues to expand his career horizons. In addition to selling cartoons to a number of magazines and syndicates, he co-owns and manages an art gallery with his beautiful wife Ginny. Film production is his ultimate goal, and he recently produced a half-hour show, "Eugene Unsolved," for a local TV station.

Jonny Hawkins

A full-time freelance cartoonist from Sherwood, Michigan, Jonny Hawkins has sold his single-panel cartoons to more than 150 different publications, including the *Saturday Evening Post*, the *National Enquirer*, and the *London Daily Mirror*. His nationally syndicated comic feature, "Hi and Jinx," appears in newspapers all over the U.S. He has had one book published, *Cheap Laughs for Church Publications*, by Baker Book House.

Gail Machlis

Gail Machlis' single-panel cartoon, "Quality Time," appears daily in newspapers across the country and is distributed by Chronicle Features Syndicate. A collection of her cartoons, *Quality Time and Other Quandaries*, was published by Chronicle Books. Her work has appeared in *Ms., Glamour, Cosmopolitan, New Woman,* and *Road and Track*, to name a few publications.

Bob Schochet

With the sale of his first cartoon to *TV Guide* in 1963, Bob Schochet began a 30-plus-year career. He's enjoyed nearly every minute of it. His work has appeared in *Good Housekeeping, Cosmopolitan, Playboy*, the *National Enquirer, Better Homes and Gardens*, and the *Wall Street Journal*, among others.

H. L. Schwadron

A resident of Ann Arbor, Michigan, H. L. Schwadron worked as a newspaper reporter and PR editor for many years, doing cartoons in his spare time. He became a full-time cartoonist in 1984. His work appears in the *Wall Street Journal*, the *Saturday Evening Post*, the *National Enquirer*, and other top publications. He also does a daily business panel, "9 to 5," which is distributed by the *Los Angeles Times* Syndicate.

John R. Shanks

John R. Shanks lives in Durham, North Carolina, with his wife Debbie and sons, Josh and Craig. He has worked in the Biochemistry Department at the University of North Carolina at Chapel Hill as a research lab technician for 17 years. He began cartooning six years ago, first appearing in the *Kappan*, the *Saturday Evening Post*, *Harvard Business Review*, and *Boy's Life*. Many other publications have also purchased his work. Besides cartooning, his passions include hiking, Felix the Cat, and his wife (not necessarily in that order).

Mike Shapiro

Mike Shapiro has been working as a freelance cartoonist for the past eight years. During that time his cartoons have appeared in many publications, including the *Wall Street Journal*, *Forbes*, *Brandweek*, the *National Law Journal*, *Cosmopolitan*, *National Review*, and *Good Housekeeping*. Mike is 34 and lives on Long Island.

Mike Twohy

Mike Twohy is a cartoonist in Kensington, California.